Beginning Anew

Reflections for Retired People

Kevin Axe

ASSISTING CHRISTIANS TO ACT

PUBLICATIONS

Beginning Anew
Reflections for Retired People
Kevin Axe

Edited by Gregory F. Augustine Pierce
Cover design by James Lemons
Typesetting by Desktop Edit Shop, Inc.

Published by: ACTA Publications
                  Assisting Christians To Act
                  4848 N. Clark Street
                  Chicago, IL 60640-4711
                  773-271-1030

Library of Congress Catalog Number: 2001098295
ISBN: 0-87946-230-2
Printed in the United States of America
Printing: 10 9 8 7 6 5 4 3 2 1
Year: 08 07 06 05 04 03 02

For Jacquie,
my best friend

Introduction

The word *retired* in much of our society implies old, worn-out, used-up, useless, frail, forgetful, rigid, opinionated, close-minded and certainly old-fashioned. We retirees (yes, I am one, although I continue to work part-time as a writer, editor and consultant) can either feed into that stereotype by adopting society's bias or we can reject that false picture of retirement by turning retirement into something new and wonderful.

For not only can we continue as growing, vibrant human beings once we stop drawing a regular workaday paycheck, but we now have a chance to make for ourselves the life we've always dreamed of.

Really, the only limitation on where we can go and what we can do is—us.

But where we choose to go and what we choose to do compete with subconscious limitations placed on us—by us.

Not only do many of the workplace "rules for life" we learned not apply once we leave the workplace, but we come to see in our later years that these "rules" probably shouldn't have been in place at all.

One workplace rule we learned, for example, was that true success in even the friendliest and most well-meaning workplace usually meant doing something better—or at least more efficiently or effectively—

than someone else. Success in life after the workplace, however, largely revolves around realizing that we simply are no better—and no worse—than anyone else. What's more, we needn't try to be.

The journey to fully embrace this deep truth about human interaction can easily fill the remainder of our days. It is a journey worth making, and we retired people are the perfect advance scouts for everyone else.

Leisure Work

Just because we no longer punch a clock or cash a regular paycheck does not mean that we retirees do no work. And I don't just mean laundry, grocery shopping, house cleaning or other domestic chores.

The way we fill the hours of the day is now our work, even if the only pay we receive is personal gratification and joy.

It's worth searching until we find the right leisure "jobs" for ourselves.

Contentment is work so engrossing that you do not know that you are working.

—Donald Hall

An Inside Job

Before we retired, we were busy, busy, busy with dozens of external details—trips, meetings, appointments, negotiations, purchases, sales, goals, revenue. All that "out there" stuff.

Now we have more time to begin to look inward, where all the action that really counts takes place: in our souls and between our ears.

Prayer is a good place to start on the "inside job."

If you can take care of the internal, you can easily take care of the external. Then you can avoid the infernal and latch on to the eternal.

—Rev. Joseph Lowery

Absolute Freedom

Okay, perhaps we're through with monthly calendars, alarm watches, pocket personal planners, weekly meetings and annual evaluations.

But those who have mapped the deep psychological forests for retirees warn us about aimless wandering in the woods.

Yes, we may do anything we want. No, we can't do everything we desire.

Absolute freedom is an oxymoron. It requires both choices and commitments.

...getting on my horse and riding off
in all directions.

—*Stephen Leacock*

What Do *You* Do?

One of the hardest challenges of retirement is the process of revising our own view of ourselves.

Many of us became near slaves to our professional personalities. When people asked us, "What do you do?" we knew they didn't mean on weekends. To a large extent, we were what we did for a living.

The journey from human *doing* to human *being* is not short or easy, but we retirees are in for trouble if we skip the trip.

I am what's I am, and that's all what's I am.

—*Popeye the Sailor*

Right...and Wrong

"I may not have too many friends...but I'm always right."

This could be the motto of too many retirees.

It's never too late for us to learn to listen more...and talk less.

Better to remain silent and be thought a fool than to speak and to remove all doubt.

—Abraham Lincoln

The Race Is Over

In the rat race of the workplace, we often had to pedal as fast as the team around us just to stay in the game.

But now that race is over, and in retirement the victory often goes to the less swift (or even the less-than-swift!).

The trouble with the rat race is that even if you win you're still a rat.

—*Lily Tomlin*

Priorities

What are the most important things in retirement? Food, shelter and clothing, of course, but then what?

Do we need sunshine year round? Trips abroad? That new car we've always coveted? Grandchildren that our children have yet to produce?

No, we need none of these to be happy. They are nice but not necessary.

Life and love are all that matter; all the rest is footnotes.

All you need is love.

—*The Beatles*

The Litany of Complaints

I know retired people who hardly ever smile. It's almost as if they define themselves by looking for the negative side of every situation.

Worse, this tendency seems to run in their families. Their gatherings become an almost endless litany of complaints about what's wrong with the world.

This sort of negative energy can, unfortunately, become addictive in retirement. We are well advised to seek out happier haunts.

Hang with happy people...and let the complainers hang by themselves.

Thoughts of disaster sustain them through the happy times.

Crisis Management

We retirees can all name a few crises in our lives that we're not sure we could endure again.

We're not even sure how we made it through them the first time, and we often shudder inwardly just remembering them.

Deep down, however, we also all know that equal crises lie ahead and that somehow we'll get through them too.

God gives us time so that everything doesn't happen at once.

Delight

Retired people are often expected to be models of somber serenity.

Unrestrained expressions of thanks, joy, pleasure or delight are sometimes frowned upon by our "more mature" contemporaries—as well as by some of the young whipper-snappers who would rather have us be seen and not heard.

Make a decision to reject such stifling restrictions.

Let the manners police—old and young alike—stew in their binding rules, regulations and face-ruining frowns.

There are really only three prayers:
"Help," "Thanks," and "Wow!"

Off Days

Even the most grounded and well-adjusted souls among us retirees have off days. We just seem at cross-purposes with everyone and everything.

And if you really want to set us off, just ask "Why so glum?"

We know that only complete idiots are happy in retirement all the time.

Maturity is a stoic response to endless reality.

—*Carrie Fisher*

Never Too Grateful

The most fortunate among us have learned through the years that a small cadre of dear friends provide the day-to-day sparks that charge our batteries, the out-stretched hands we grab onto, the ever-available shoulders we cry on.

There's no way to ever be too grateful for them.

True friendship is a plant of slow growth,
and must undergo and withstand
the shocks of adversity
before it is entitled
to the appellation.

—*George Washington*

By the Numbers

One of the most threatening elements of many work lives is the tyranny of "the numbers."

"You've had a fairly good year. Your staff seems happy. No one complains about you. But you just did not make your numbers."

No bonus; no promotion; no kidding.

But that is the game; and if you don't like it you get off the playing field. Many of us did.

Not everything that can be counted counts,
and not everything that counts
can be counted.

—*Albert Einstein*

No Limit

The very act of retirement signals a somewhat final choice. Oh, volunteer work or part-time jobs may follow, but the major carousel of professional life has come to a halt.

Then the work of retirement begins. We begin to lead the lives we've always envisioned and to look for final meaning in all that came before.

At last we have the leisure to love others without limit—of time, of effort, of attention, of commitment. For now we recognize that things will come to an end, and we have to choose how to spend the rest of what we have.

Not to decide is to decide.

—Harvey Cox

Getting to Know You

The longer we live, the more we discover what we have in common with other people—if we have the courage to really let others get to know us, that is.

But many of us skim through retired life surrounded by a psychological twelve-foot wall, convinced that if others don't know us they can't dislike or hurt us.

In retirement we have both the time and the opportunity to get to know others on a much deeper, more fulfilling level. But to do that we've got to share who we really are, and that is easier said than done.

What is often thought to be the most personal is often universal.

—*Carl Rogers*

I Can't Fix You

Many of us retired folk think we are expert human caretakers. "Just do as I say," we insist, "and you'll be fine."

But most people are not looking for us to fix them. What they want is someone to listen to them, to share their joys and sufferings, to accept them for who and what they are.

Often when we are trying to fix others, we are really trying to protect ourselves from being vulnerable or getting involved.

By trying to fix you with advice, rather
than simply suffering with you,
I hold myself away
from your pain.

—*Parker Palmer*

The Big Mo

Sports commentators go on and on about momentum (the "Big Mo") and how important it is for a team to prevail in sports.

But we retirees experience the same phenomenon in our personal lives. Some days we hit personal home runs without even trying; other days we can't even crawl to first base.

Luckily, in retirement no one is keeping score or rating our achievements except ourselves, and we are free to cut ourselves some slack.

Sometimes you take baseball so seriously you miss out on the fun of the game.

—Rick Dempsey

Goodbye to All That

One of the hardest chores throughout our years in the workforce was getting along with certain kinds of co-workers. No matter how hard we tried, some folks seemed determined to cause us problems whenever they got the chance.

Goodbye to all that.

This quiet freedom from aggravation is what makes retirement a God-given grace.

I have reached the time of my life
when I don't have to work
with anyone who is not happy
to work with me.

—*Sir George Solti*

If Only

Some of us retired people like to play "If only...."

"If only I lived where the sun shines year round..." or "If only I lived near my kids..." or "If only there were a golf course nearby...."

Maybe it's time to get up and go!

Except that no matter where we go, we can't leave ourselves behind. The most important destinations are internal.

My life is more affected by what I dwell on than by what I dwell in.

Prayer and Miracles

Those of us retired folk who have spent serious time in our lives asking God for things in prayer often wonder just how the whole process works.

Is God even aware that we're praying? Is God sitting somewhere monitoring six billion computer screens, keeping tabs on each of our thoughts, words and deeds? Is God intimately involved in our lives—granting this, withholding that? And, if so, aren't we just God's divine playthings?

No one really knows how prayer works, of course; but some of us know—really know—that it does.

We have experienced too many miracles in our lives to doubt it.

Coincidence is merely a miracle in which God wishes to remain anonymous.

Birds of the Air

Perhaps the most reassuring passage in all the Scriptures has Jesus' urging us to look at the birds of the air that are cared for by their heavenly Father for doing absolutely nothing, at least in the areas of toiling or reaping.

They almost sound as if they are retired!

We retirees can aspire to this sort of easy-come, easy-go detachment and maybe even practice it most of the time.

Worry adds no value to our days.

Anxiety does not empty tomorrow of its sorrow—only today of its strength.

—*Charles A. Spurgeon*

Seething Silence

Sometimes we retired people become masters of the unspoken word. Our facial expressions and body language can wound a relationship just as surely as harsh words.

"I didn't say anything," we claim in a self-righteous tone of voice, but our continued refusal to discuss what is going on speaks volumes.

Although there are times when silence is golden, other times it is fool's gold.

The cruelest lies are often told in silence.

—*Robert Louis Stevenson*

Live Till You Die

I once had a college professor who took up snow skiing at age seventy-four, just as he was finally about to retire.

After observing him, I've made up my mind that there is almost nothing I'll ever be too old to do, or at least try, in retirement.

Even if we retired people don't have the physical strength and stamina of thirty or forty years ago, we should refuse to put ourselves (or let others put us) in an "age-appropriate" box.

God willing, we ought to live till we die. And God is willing! Are we?

God, keep me green and growing.

Inner and Outer Children

Retirement is often the time to begin processing our lives in a way that helps us understand who we are and how we want to be remembered.

Some of us try to nurture our neglected "inner child." Others of us, often at our dear ones' urgings, keep on trying to control our "outer child."

Either way, the examined life can make a thousand tomorrows better.

Life can be understood only backwards, but it must be lived forwards.

—*Sören Kierkegaard*

Locked Minds

We retired people, despite our freedom, often become more rigidly set in our ways and thoughts than the nine-to-five crowd we left behind with all their schedules, rules and alarm clocks.

But a locked mind provides a phony sort of emotional security.

Locked minds shut out new thoughts and the people who speak them, and closed-minded people gradually retreat into a lonely island of self-righteousness and fear.

Open the door and throw away the key.

The world is full of lonely people, all isolated in a private, secret dungeon.

—*Loretta Girzartis*

Neither Credit Nor Blame

Every convict on death row is somebody's kid.

Luckily, most of us older parents have escaped such tearful turmoil. Our kids may not be Einsteins, but they often make us proud.

Less fortunate parents need our support and understanding. They may be no more guilty of their adult children's crimes than we are responsible for our adult children's continuing success.

Remember: We retirees are not our children, but neither are our children us.

A child shall not suffer for the iniquity
of a parent, nor a parent suffer
for the iniquity of a child;
the righteousness of the righteous
shall be his own,
and the wickedness of the wicked
shall be his own.

—*Ezekiel* 18:20

The Best Argument

A friend taught me a little human-relations trick that works wonders in retirement.

When we're engaged in a spirited conversation, sometimes the tone can begin to turn nasty. At that point, rather than lay our best verbal shot on our adversary we should pause, count inwardly to five (or more, if necessary) before we speak each time.

Likely as not, the other person, awash in silence, begins to backpedal, slow down, calm down, and become more reasonable and less agitated.

It's worth a try.

At times, just plain silence reveals an excellent command of the English language.

Whoopee!

Who says age-appropriate behavior needs to be bor-ing?

If an activity or pastime sounds good, try it.

Who says retirement has to be retiring?

Those who are mentally and emotionally
healthy are those who have learned
when to say yes and when to say no
and when to say whoopee!

—*Willard S. Krabill*

Grumpy

Some of us think retirement comes with an unexpiring license to complain.

"You'd gripe, too, if your knees hurt like mine."

But if we focus on the positive, we improve our attitude and our whole mood.

And a positive attitude is wildly contagious.

**Some days I wake up grumpy;
some days I just let him sleep.**

One of These Days

One of the most effective advertising slogans I've ever seen came from the U. S. Army: "Be All That You Can Be."

Who would disagree with that goal in life? And in retirement we finally have the time to pursue it.

To help speed up the process even more, the super bookstores have massive racks of self-improvement books, many of them aimed at retired people.

But these plans usually recommend too much, too fast. They seem to ignore the fact that if you're going to eat an elephant it's best to proceed one bite at a time.

Self-change reads easy but happens hard.

Avoiding Unpleasantries

It may take us months—even years—into retirement to realize that we rarely need to fight anyone, anymore, about anything.

We've got the time to wait for a situation to change, to find an alternative source or place to do business, to go about things in a way that minimizes conflict.

It's up to us to decide how we are going to operate in order to avoid unpleasant scenes and people.

Life is short, and we have not too much
time for gladdening the hearts
of those who travel with us.
Oh, be swift to love!
Make haste to be kind.

—*Journal of Henri Frederic Amiel*

Non-Smothering Retirement

In *The Prophet*, Kahlil Gibran urges married folks to "let the winds of the heavens dance between you."

When a couple have been apart for about half their weekday hours for most of their lives, the snugly dream of retirement togetherness can become troubled sleep, if not a nightmare, if they don't watch out.

If every waking minute of every day is a shared experience, what's left to share?

One thing we should probably have learned from our pre-retirement days is that it's probably a good idea to plan some spaces in our togetherness.

In a good marriage, we become custodians of each other's solitude.

—*Johann Wolfgang von Goethe*

Fatigued Advice

Despite our freedom to just sit and stare, to take slow walks around the neighborhood, to take a nap whenever we want, we retired folk don't seem to last late into the night the way we used to.

Often our grown children don't seem to understand that we often become more cranky and impatient—not to mention less clear-headed—as the clock ticks on. We may not be up for giving (or receiving) life-changing advice or participating in heavy discussions as the hours grow late.

Never make an important decision or give any advice after nine o'clock at night.

When we are tired, we are attacked by ideas
we conquered long ago.

—*Friedrich Nietzsche*

Honk If You Love God

Sometimes when I'm walking down the street, a friend driving by honks and waves. The warm glow I get from that simple interaction can last for hours.

I've discovered I can communicate with God in the same way. I don't need incense and dark churches and candlelight to pray, though these work fine too.

But I like praying as I go about my daily "business of retirement." It's like honking and waving at God.

**It's no use walking to do our praying
unless our walking is our praying.**

Friends

Whole libraries could be filled with books about friendship, and one of the hardest decisions in retirement is whether to move away and leave old friends behind.

There's no easy answer, nor even a correct one.

What is sure is that we need good friends, whether old or new.

I awoke this morning with devout thanksgiving for my friends, the old and the new.

—*Ralph Waldo Emerson*

Bad Day

At times we retirees fall victim to self-pity. Are we really having a bad day, or have we had a couple trying moments that we have nursed and squeezed for all the sympathy they are worth?

If we label a day bad, likely as not we'll continue to make sure it is.

And if we really want to prove how bad it is, we try to inflict it on others around us so that we can cause a "group bad day."

Hint: We can start a new day at any minute of any hour. No need to wait until midnight.

Mood swing: when you try to swing someone with your mood.

The Gift of Giving

Many of us retired folks actively care for our failing parents or other relatives or friends. This is a labor of willing but often difficult love.

But we get by giving—whether to our children, grandchildren, aging parents, friends or even to absolute strangers.

And only when we stop giving do we realize that we are no longer receiving the greatest gift of all...the gift of giving.

Then it is probably time for us to seek out someone else in need.

**Whoever does the will of my Father in heaven
is my brother and sister and mother.**

—Matthew 12:50

The Best Medicine

With more time on our hands in retirement, it pays to maintain our ability to laugh.

I mean to really laugh—big, fat, belly laughs, laughter that brings tears to our eyes.

Belly laughs keep us grounded and young at heart. They are a sign of total letting go, of total comfort with fellow human beings.

Love makes the world go around,
but laughter keeps us
from getting dizzy.

I Dunno

"So, what do you think of gun control?" "Abortion?" "Gays in the military?" "Capital punishment?" "The war on terrorism?"

Before retirement, we lived full and varied lives, packed with experience and reflection. It's only right that we share the fruits of our wisdom with all comers.

But true wisdom contains a healthy dash of true humility.

It is always the secure who are humble.

—*G. K. Chesterton*

The Habit of Changing Habits

Over the years we all settle on preferred ways to do almost everything. (Just try starting your shopping at the other end of the supermarket to see what I mean.)

This is good. No one wants or needs to reinvent the wheel every single day. And good habits are the basis of all virtue.

But habits also prevent us from continuing to grow. Perhaps the only way to keep from getting too predictable in our retirement is to predict that we will! Then we can fight like hell to make sure it doesn't happen.

Want to change your life?
Change your habits.

Hear, Hear

By and large, we learn more when we're listening than when we're talking.

But many of us still prefer to talk.

I've heard it said that God gave us two ears and one mouth because we're supposed to listen twice as much as we speak.

Maybe we retired folk should try it.

Let him listen diligently, very diligently.

—Isaiah 21:7

What, Me Worry?

An aging wag once reflected that parents of grown children are typically just about as happy as their least-happy grown child. That's a special threat to us with more time on our hands in retirement.

We pray; we worry; we obsess. Should we call our kids? Should we give advice? When will the work of parenting ever end?

An even wiser wag noted that the antidote to such addictive, mind-numbing worry is to put a harness on your consciousness. Either go do something about the problem or banish it from your mind.

Those who torment themselves
with eagerness and anxiety
do little, and that badly.

—*St. Francis de Sales*

Hurry Up and Wait

One of the small but very welcome benefits of being retired is to be able to go to stores when there are no crowds. Another is to drive leisurely on normally jammed streets and freeways.

So when we do get stuck in traffic or a long line, we should just cool our jets. After all, perhaps for the first time in our adult lives, we usually don't have to be anywhere in a big hurry.

We could consider using the waiting time to pray for our loved ones.

After all, they might not have the time to pray for themselves that day.

What to do when it rains?
Let it!

Chronic Pain

Whether it be muscles, joints, bones, skin or organs—someday something in us will start to make its weakness terribly obvious to us. Then we've joined the ranks of the chronic-pain sufferers. Most of us do not experience major-league pain or disabling pain, perhaps, but we do live with discomfort that we know will be with us until the day we die.

As always, we have choices. Do we ignore the pain in the hope it will go away, check out suggested ways to live with it, or spend half our remaining life complaining about it to anyone who will listen?

What we attend to we will become, and we are more than our pain. Pain is inevitable; misery is optional.

**I lighten my pain by the joys
that come from virtue.**

—*4 Maccabees* 9:31

The Dream Machine

My late mother was hopelessly hooked on "winning the big one." Cars, homes, vacations, lotteries—any pitch that arrived in the mail—got her attention.

Her logic was simple and powerful: Someone's going to win, so why not me?

She was a constant, tireless dream machine. As she neared death, Mom would actually worry about how she'd divide up her prospective "winnings."

Of course, she never won much; but the expense never went much beyond postage stamps. So where was the harm?

**Most times we already have what we need.
The challenge is to want what we have.**

Retired Organizers

Solitary soldiers rarely do much damage to an enemy. You've got to have at least a small platoon to mount any sort of credible charge.

And so it is in our neighborhoods and communities. If we retirees become solitary troublemakers, we will soon run out of ammo and be forced to give up our lonely fight.

But we've got the time to become community leaders, to organize our neighbors, to create instruments of justice and peace in our towns and neighborhoods.

I will die like a true-blue rebel. Don't waste any time in mourning—organize.

—*Joe Hill*

The Good with the Bad

Some of us retirees carry reminders of our mortality around with us everywhere we go.

I happen to have titanium knees, a result of miracle surgery that lets me walk and climb stairs with no pain whatsoever.

They also make for wild times at airport metal-detector checkpoints in these days of heightened security.

So we just have to take the good with the bad...and keep our sense of humor intact.

And if I laugh at any mortal thing,
'Tis that I may not weep.

—*Lord Byron*

A Friend Indeed

We retirees all fight our daily battles, inward and outward, and we do need one special friend to lean on. Just as much, we need someone to lean on us.

A true friendship is an adventure in grace—one of mutual trust, openness, comfort.

A person without a close friend is truly destitute, and a destitute is anyone without a close friend.

I have always felt that the great high privilege, relief, and comfort of friendship was that one had to explain nothing.

—*Katherine Mansfield*

Telephone Calls

Phone calls are by nature somewhat intrusive to retired people. They tend to interrupt what we're doing, even if we're really not doing all that much. And if our knees creak or bones crack as we go to answer the phone, the caller is already in a bit of trouble in our minds.

Moreover, if we're the kind who usually expect the worst, we're always a bit stressed already as we pick up the phone.

It's good to remind ourselves that a phone call merely means some human being wants to talk with us...and for that we should be thankful (unless, of course, it's a telemarketer).

Why don't I see you anymore? Did I disappoint you? Did you call me one night to say you were in trouble and hear a tone in my voice that made you say you were just fine?

—*Garrison Keillor*

Scattered Feathers

A grade-school teacher once told me, "When you tell lies or carry tales about others, it's like ripping open a feather pillow on a windy mountain top. You can try for the rest of your life, but you'll never retrieve all the feathers."

Sticks and stones may break somebody's bones, but harmful words can last forever.

With more time for talking in retirement, it's worth remembering that gossip is a good habit to squelch.

How long will I have to pay for just a handful of tossed-off words?

—*Anne Tyler*

Skipping Through Galilee

Perhaps the funniest part of the Scriptures is when Jesus is popping up all over Galilee after he rose from the dead.

Passing through walls, appearing out of nowhere, surprising and nearly "scaring the bejesus" out of everyone.

Once we hang up the nine-to-five shtick, we too can pop up in unexpected places—delighting, supporting and comforting those around us.

Lord, make me a walking, talking, surprising instrument of your peace in my retirement.

Betrayed?

We have all experienced betrayal at some point in our work lives. We've been cheated, slandered, disappointed, lied to.

Each passing year of our career taught us the hard lesson of self-protection: In the end, you can't really trust anyone.

So in our retirement, we retreat into our castles, lock the doors, and pull the blinds.

Unless, of course, we'd rather be happy.

It is happier to be sometimes cheated than not to trust.

—Samuel Johnson

Snail Mail

Despite omnipresent cell phones, cheap long-distance phone rates, and the instant outreach of internet e-mail, most of us retirees still delight in receiving an old-fashioned letter in the mailbox.

There's a certain loving concern and thoughtfulness that travels the miles from writer to reader in a letter that just doesn't attach to an e-mail or even a phone call.

And the love is not lessened by the time between sending and receiving.

Write and send a letter to a loved one today.

To write a letter is to be alone
with my thoughts
in the conjured presence
of another person.

—*John Bayley*

That Reminds Me

Many of us retirees who like to talk need continuing education in good listening.

People come up to us and share a matter of some importance. We listen briefly and then start to open our mouth before they've finished two sentences. We may even help them finish their second sentence.

It rarely occurs to us that they are not impressed that we have a similar experience—or even a better one—to shoot right back at them. In fact, maybe they just wanted to tell us something without looking for a response from us at all.

Some of the most supportive people I know spend a lot of time just nodding their heads.

People want to know how much you care before they care how much you know.

"By Purpose"

Perhaps my family's favorite language oddity has been the enshrined phrase "She (or he) did it by purpose." This phrase first characterized a one-year-old's slap of a five-year-old (at least according to the five-year-old), but it became a way of everyone in my family differentiating between intentional and accidental actions.

We retirees need to be careful of the injuries we cause others "by purpose."

There will be plenty of harm we do by accident, but we can minimize the intentional ones.

Who's sorry now?

—*Patsy Cline*

Bittersweet Sorrow

As our lives get rearranged in retirement, distance inevitably comes between us and former work friends and associates.

We can't say "goodbye to all that" without saying goodbye to most of them too. Whether it's a distance of miles, lifestyles, interests or just available time (yes, even in retirement), the absence of our former colleagues on a day-to-day basis can create at least small holes in our souls.

So while we might be glad that we have left the nine-to-five grind, we might be a little sad that we have left some people we care about behind.

Grief is the tax humans pay
for loving one another.

—*Bill Moyers*

How Grand?

Grandchildren are frequently the prize topic of conversation among retirees. "Ask me about my grandchildren," reads the popular bumper sticker on many a Winnebago.

When we retirees no longer have deadlines or sales goals or corporate intrigue to occupy our minds, it's easy to start living vicariously through our busy kids or grandkids.

God bless them, but do we really want to spend the greatest part of our retirement talking mostly about them?

We need to get, and keep, a life of our own.

**St. Peter is going to ask about us,
not our grandchildren.**

The Long Goodbye

Many of us retired folk struggle with Alzheimer's disease. To watch a parent, spouse, close friend or family member slip away with this maddening illness can be more painful for the watchers than the watched. I've heard it called "the long goodbye."

But when my wife and I went through it for a couple years with her mother, wonderful guides taught us to seek out and treasure the positive and ignore the rest.

"Praise her for what she can do, and ignore what she can no longer do," they advised.

This was God-sent guidance, and now I share it with you.

**I do not capture understanding;
it captures me.**

Greener Grass

Why can't we all have the life of travel, security, good looks, good health and overall well-being of some of our neighbors?

One of life's hardest lessons is to quit comparing ourselves to others. We set a sure trap for ourselves when we persist in comparing our insides to their outsides.

If one only wished to be happy, this could easily be accomplished; but we wish to be happier than other people, and this is always difficult, for we believe others to be happier than they are.

—*Charles de Secondat Montesquieu*

Bad Chemistry

One of life's continuing mysteries is why we get along with some folks and not with others.

Back in the workplace, the rule seemed to be· Get along and go along if you want to get ahead. In retirement we have no such rule, and just getting along often shows itself to be the often-uneasy truce it has always been.

Maybe in retirement we should just avoid those people we really can't stand. It's a luxury we've earned.

I don't think you can analyze why in hell it is
you can get on with one person
and you can't with another.

—*Katharine Hepburn*

Get a Wiggle On

Those of us looking to extend the length of our retirement (and our lives) need options for, not excuses from, exercise.

For safe, weather-resistant, non-boring exercise, buy yourself a cheap, adjustable drafting table. Extend the height of it as far as it will go and place it over the front wheel of an exercise bike. Then sit and pedal while you read the newspaper, work a puzzle, watch TV, draw a masterpiece or play solitaire.

The secret to exercise is to distract ourselves while we do it.

Use it or lose it.

Fresh Starts

Broken marriages, broken families, and broken relationships (not to mention simply being broke!) can sometimes all but sink us in retirement.

We have to use our willpower to recover hope. The future is ours to make, but only if we take the necessary steps.

We need to pray for the serenity to accept what we cannot change, the courage to change what we are able, and the wisdom to know the difference.

You may have a fresh start any moment you choose; for this thing that we call "failure" is not the falling down, but the staying down.

—*Mary Pickford*

Make a Difference

President John F. Kennedy used to talk frequently about the duty of citizens to make a contribution to society. This certainly—and maybe especially—includes us retired people.

As retirees, we certainly have a right to our well-deserved and long-awaited rest and recreation. But many of us who have been retired for a while realize that we often get bored with leisure activity alone. We need something we can sink our teeth (even if they are false!) into.

Life has more meaning when we help make a difference in the world. We might visit the homebound or those in nursing homes, for example, or tutor a needy child or tend a civic garden. At the very least, we can continue in the tradition of so many previous retirees by writing letters to the editor and to elected officials on issues we care about deeply.

Everyone can't do everything. But the
difference between doing nothing
and doing something is enormous.

—*Daniel Berrigan, S.J.*

Noise Addicts

TVs, Walkmans, CD players, DVDs, surround sound, woofers, tweeters, MP3.

For many of us retirees, these gadgets are a few of our favorite toys—and they get better every year.

But just for kicks, at least for us noise addicts, it's good to turn off the sound now and then. Few life-changing insights or life-enhancing thoughts can fight their way through the din of the world's greatest hits—even if they are sung by Sinatra or Streisand.

All miseries derive from not being able to sit quietly in a room alone.

—Blaise Pascal

Righteous Indignation

Whenever we retirees are tempted to pick up the phone or walk up to someone and give him or her a heated piece of our mind, it's probably good to take a different tack.

Not only will the heat overpower whatever light our opinion might shed, but the blisters engendered by the exchange will afflict both parties for a long time to come.

Understatement usually speaks louder than screams.

Tact is the knack of making a point
without making an enemy.

—*Howard W. Newton*

See the Light

People recovering from addictions know the terrible power of the mind to deny reality, to play fatal tricks in the service of self-destruction.

Sometimes true insight, even wisdom, for us retirees seems to come out of the blue. Or maybe we finally "hear" what people have been trying to tell us for a long time.

It is then that we have to both see the light and make the changes necessary to stay in that light.

The need for change bulldozed a road down the center of my mind.

—*Maya Angelou*

True Believers

Religion is a many splendored thing: guiding, challenging, empowering and supporting untold millions of adherents throughout most of human history. We retirees often find a special comfort in our religious beliefs as retirement gives us more time for spiritual thoughts and practices.

Each religion paints a picture of God according to its own particular theology. But often these God-fearing religions relegate nonbelievers in their beliefs to some form of outcast netherworld.

I've always had trouble with a God who is more interested in exclusion than inclusion.

The God who would damn,
say, Anne Frank or Gandhi
for not being Christian
isn't worth worshipping.

—*John Garvey*

Re-Tired

The very word *retired* spells out one of the firm realities of retirement.

We retirees are almost always tired at night, often tired in the afternoon, and occasionally even tired as soon as we arise in the morning. It goes with the territory.

That's all the more reason for us to make adequate rest a prime principle of retirement.

Try this on your loved ones: "Dear, we love you beyond words; but please don't call after ten at night unless someone's dying or the house is on fire."

To sleep: perchance to dream:
ay, there's the rub.

—*William Shakespeare*

Surprise!

For years, vigilant parents have made resistant kids wear jackets and boots in bad weather lest they "catch a death of cold."

Then smart-aleck kids began coming home from school with printouts from the internet claiming there is no connection at all between winter colds and winter weather.

In the same way, we have been told all our lives that retirement means that we stop work and drop out of active life.

Then we come up with the stories of such "retirees" as Bob Hope, Billy Graham, Mother Teresa and the multi-retired Michael Jordan.

Much of what makes life worth living lies beyond the realm of provable fact.

—*Madeleine L'Engle*

Happy Talk

Perhaps one of the greatest blessings of retirement is just being with good friends. We needn't spend time inwardly judging ourselves or planning carefully what we might say next. Time with friends is a feast of mutual acceptance.

And if we do express different points of view no one feels personally rejected or attacked.

It makes us want to schedule the next get together before the current visit ends.

The happiest conversation is that of which nothing is distinctly remembered but a general effect of pleasing impression.

—*Samuel Johnson*

Ruin Your Day

Some of the most popular radio and TV talk shows are fueled by one main element: folks who spout totally opposite opinions, whether they make sense or not. Reasoned discussion and attempts at compromise are scarce in these arenas.

The fare of the day for this kind of "entertainment" is name-calling and distortion of opponents' views.

Some of us can get hooked on this kind of stuff in retirement because the demon of negative excitement always beckons. "Hey, you," it calls. "Get involved in this manufactured conflict and really ruin your day."

I never make the mistake of arguing
with people for whose opinions
I have no respect.

—*Edward Gibbon*

Busybodies?

As we retirees walk through life, we see all kinds of problems around us: potholes in the streets, broken tree limbs hanging dangerously over neighbors' homes, people smacking their kids around in public places, maybe even someone shoplifting from a store.

How do we decide when—and if—to get involved?

One guideline should come from a variant of the golden rule: Always get involved with others when you would want others to get involved with you...and keep your nose out of things you'd want others to keep their noses out of.

You shall love your neighbor as yourself.

—*Leviticus 19:18*

Accentuate the Positive

Have you ever noticed the expression on others' faces when we suggest how they might improve themselves? Do we really think they don't already know their faults and are just sitting around waiting for us to bring their failings and weaknesses to their attention before correcting them?

On the other hand, if we retirees can find ways to genuinely praise others, maybe they'll get motivated to work more productively toward progress in areas in which they really need it.

I have found that I can never make anyone better by criticism—except myself.

Automotive Angst

All right. We say we're finally beginning to get it all together—through prayer, meditation, communing with nature or just getting a good night's sleep. We begin to experience the serenity we sought when we retired.

Then we cheerfully slide behind the steering wheel of our car and very soon expose ourselves to the antics of the world's biggest nitwits. "How can idiots like that keep their licenses?" we want to know.

Horns honk. Curses fly. Turn signals blink or don't blink. Tires screech. Fingers communicate.

Suddenly, we're back in the emotional space we retired to escape.

Take a deep breath, slowly exhale.
This too shall pass.

Friendly Strangers

In the hectic, pell-mell, workaday lives most of us have led before retirement, dozens of people we used to see every day served almost as human wallpaper in our lives. Not only did we not connect with them as fellow human beings, we moved about as if they were not even there.

But now that we are retired, why do we stand silently in line behind a stranger at the theater? Why don't we engage a clerk at the grocery in some friendly chatter? What's wrong with stopping and speaking with people we see in the park as we walk our dogs?

We don't want to be the kind of retirees that talk people's arms and legs off, of course, but even a brief human connection can make someone's day just a bit brighter—including our own.

**Be kind. Everyone we meet
is fighting a hard battle.**

Meet You Half Way

One-sided friendships (even marriages) often cap-size in retirement: "Hey, I did my part. I pulled my weight. Now it's his (or her) turn."

That very act of measurement often dooms the relationship. True love doesn't count the costs or measure results. There are no sides; there is no parity; there can be no scales.

In relationships, two halves do not make a whole.

On Slowing Down

The pace of our former workplaces usually had three speeds: fast, faster and faster still.

No wonder it takes many of us months, even years, to begin to slow down after our retirement.

But eventually, we all learn that it is okay just to watch the grass grow or to stop and smell those roses we've been speeding by all our lives.

Slow down, you move too fast.

—Paul Simon

Some Body

No matter how well we care for ourselves in retirement, at some point our body parts begin to wear out.

We're in better shape than some friends, worse than others.

Ironically, we're sometimes tempted to avoid friends who are struggling physically, rather than warmly embracing them. Not only do we flee their pain, but subconsciously we may even blame them for their illness or disability.

Retirement is a time to actively connect with others, rather than reject or isolate them.

Do not mistake illness for evil.

Quivering-Lip Courage

Who can forget the courage of the passengers who fought the terrorists over Pennsylvania on 9/11/01—crashing their plane but saving the lives of countless others on the ground?

They were undoubtledly afraid, but they somehow found the courage to act—even if their lips were quivering with fear as they did.

Most of us retired folk will never be asked to be that brave. But we do need to overcome our fear of growing old.

Courage is the strength to move ahead despite the fear.

One-Sided Nostalgia

"Those were the days...." "They don't make things like they used to...." "Back in my day...." "When I was your age...." And the beat goes on.

Nostalgia is one-sided. It only remembers the good stuff. Contrarians even go so far as to say that "the good old days" simply never existed. At a minimum, they weren't the romantic paradise depicted in our memories.

Remember, the same folks who rode in the horse-drawn sleighs with bells-a-jingle also had to go out in the snow to the outhouse to empty the chamber pots every morning.

Not only can rose-colored memory distort the past; it can also unfairly diminish the present.

Don't let ol' folks tell you about the good ol' days. I was there. Where was they at?

—*Jackie "Moms" Mabley*

Resentment

Perhaps the most harmful emotion for those of us who are retired is the unchecked force of resentment.

Resentment, from the Latin to "feel anew," can last a lifetime and often just grows stronger with age.

Time does not, alas, heal all wounds. Years, even decades, later we can still relive those maddening moments, feel that delicious anger, send mental hand grenades to those who did us wrong. Yet these people don't even know we're thinking of them. They're simply living—rent-free and awareness-free—in our minds, day after day, month after month, year after resentment-filled year.

Especially in retirement, we need to quell all these spirit-killing feelings.

**Resentment is an acid that eats
its own container.**

Precious Togetherness

The dream of most retired married folks is to grow old gracefully together.

Perhaps we plan to drive around the country and experience new people and places. Or maybe we just want to stay at home and relax after decades of hard work.

The reality, however, is that sooner or later our life-long love will be interrupted—sometimes gradually over a long illness, sometimes suddenly with an unexpected death.

That makes today's togetherness all the more precious.

Love—why I'll tell you what love is: it's you at 75 and her at 71, each of you listening for the other's step in the next room, each afraid that a sudden silence, a sudden cry, could mean a lifetime's talk is over.

—*Brian Moore*

What's It All About?

After we retire, many of us try to bring more meaning to the daily events in our lives. Whether through religion, reading, support groups, or just deep talks with friends—we search for ultimate answers.

But often the underlying meaning of life has a way of arriving when we least expect it, rather than as a result of any systematic search for enlightenment.

Sometimes we need to slow down, relax, and listen—not with our ears, but with our hearts.

Often it is not the events in our lives that bring meaning, but the space between the events.

Discretion

Even the most honest retirees in the world frequently struggle between what we know to be fact and what we choose to say to others.

Sometimes the facts would help others, as when we know someone missed a child's college graduation because of a chemotherapy appointment, but we promised not to disclose the cancer.

Other times the facts would hurt others, as when we know for a fact someone is committing adultery, but we don't feel it is our place to disclose the cheating.

Discretion is sometimes a necessary part of retired life.

The better part of valor is discretion.

—*Shakespeare*

Trapped

The rat race is perhaps the most common metaphor for the nine-to-five world of business and commerce. It was, is, and probably always will be a world of contest and competition, with thousands of daily winners and losers.

The more fortunate among us "won" often enough to be able to say goodbye to the contest, to quit competing with our colleagues in order to survive. Others rarely win and must compete for a lifetime, even into old age, in order to survive.

If only they recognized their blessings.

—*Virgil*

Healthy Hobbies

In retirement, hobbies can easily slide into obsessions.

Okay, so what exactly is the difference between a healthy hobby and an all-consuming obsession?

Is it just a matter of degree or how much time and money we spend on a particular activity? Or is it rather how attached we become to the pursuit of that activity? Or is it a question of what deeper values are we avoiding or sacrificing in the service (slavery?) of our favorite pastime?

Healthy hobbies are ones that we can take or leave.

You can never get enough of what you
don't need to make you happy.

—*Eric Hoffer*

Packrats

Some of us are lifelong packrats—like the oldster with the shoebox in the attic labeled "string too short to save."

"Stuff" just seems to pile up in retirement: financial records, family photos, unread books and magazines, souvenirs, knickknacks, clothes, etc., etc.

Almost without realizing it, we find ourselves presiding over bulging closets and chests, our minds busy scheming to protect it all with electronic-surveillance devices.

The one-year rule may be a pretty good guide to eliminating "stuff": If we haven't touched it in a year, it's safe to get rid of it (all except the photos, that is).

That which you share will multiply;
that which you withhold will diminish.

As Good As We Are

I've heard it said that some true contemplatives and mystics reach a point where they have absolutely no fear of death.

For the rest of us, especially as we visit more and more friends in hospitals and later bid them farewell at funerals, death begins to hover ever more closely in the background. And the closer it gets, the more frightened we become.

The only way to truly conquer the fear of death is to hold hands with those we love.

Everybody knows everybody's dying.
That's why people are as good as they are.

—*Mark Harris*

Forgive Me

When we offend others, we often apologize. We say, "I'm sorry," and then get on with life.

But if we also add "Please forgive me," the interaction can be much more meaningful.

The offended one gets a chance to grow, too, by saying "I forgive you."

In the inner act of forgiveness people
first surrender the right to get even.
They cease defining the one or ones
who hurt them in terms
of the hurt that was caused.

—*Louis Smedes*

Rear Vision

Life is uncertain—perhaps never more so than since terrorism reared its ugly head in our world. Prudent retired people keep a watchful eye in all directions.

But we can allow our prudence to overwhelm our common sense. All of life involves risk, and we can't spend all our time protecting our lives or we'll have no time to live our lives.

Yes, we can be too safe.

Too many people go through life running from things that aren't chasing them.

Downsizing Our Desires

There's an old saying that the poor don't know they're poor and the rich don't know they're rich.

But we all experience rising expectations. Once we have air conditioning in our cars, for example, we'd never be without it. Luxuries become necessities; desires become needs.

Retirement, however, is a good time to begin to scale down both our possessions and our wants. This frees us from taking care of things. It reduces our upkeep expenses on things we rarely use. And it allows us to pass things on to others who will cherish them or who need them more than we do.

You can't take it with you.

Taps

There is perhaps no more haunting melody than the trumpeted *Taps* that is played to sign off on daily activities or to lower the flag—or a coffin.

Taps will be played for each of us some day—sooner for some than for others, but for each of us nonetheless.

Our job in retirement is to enjoy the years we have left, realizing that they are limited and abundant at the same time.

May He support us all the day long, till the
shades lengthen, and the evening comes,
and the busy world is hushed, and the fever
of life is over, and our work is done.
Then in His mercy may He give us
safe lodging and a holy rest,
and peace at the last.

—*John Henry Newman*

Sorrow Times

Not one retired person lives completely in a land of milk and honey. Let's face it, bowls of cherries are sometimes reduced to pits. We often wonder why, oh why, this or that is happening to us.

We retirees know all about the valleys of life—the emergency rooms and hospices, the funeral homes and graveside goodbyes, the broken hearts and broken families.

Some days even our God seems so very, very far away.

Of course, God is always right there, working through our family and friends and the kindness of strangers.

God's will never sends us where
God's grace does not reach.

The Wisdom to Let Go

In some cultures retired folk are revered for their experience and wisdom. They're even called "elders" in the sense of "wise older people."

In our culture that respect is no longer as widespread as it once was.

Perhaps the proper response is for those of us who are retired to give our opinion, offer our advice...and then detach with love and acceptance.

"Let go and let God," as they say in Alcoholics Anonymous.

Hold the reins lightly.
See everything.
Correct some of it.
Forget the rest of it.

—*Pope John XXIII*

Setting Others in Our Ways

Although we retired people are not as systematically programmed as the computers we've come to love and/or hate, we're still pretty set in our ways.

And we are often only too willing to show others the "right" way to do and think about things. The problem is, they aren't always all that grateful for our "help."

A big step forward comes when we quit trying to control others. Quite often the boundaries of our attempts to control cannot be controlled themselves.

Nothing so needs reforming
as other people's habits.

—*Mark Twain*

A Confession

They say it's harder to talk about one's prayer life than one's sex life.

So here goes: In mid-marriage, my wife and I began to say short prayers together at various times during the day. We have continued and intensified this practice in retirement. And we have great prayer.

I hope I haven't scandalized you too much!

There are few men who would dare publish to the world the prayers they make to almighty God.

—*Michel de Montaigne*

Wounded Healing

Some spiritual gurus say that the twelve-step program, begun in the United States in the 1930s, will go down in history as the greatest contribution of the western world to the practice of spirituality.

The key to twelve-step programs such as Alcoholics Anonymous is the simple idea that the process of one sufferer talking with another can slowly, slowly, slowly heal them both (through the grace of a "higher power" that each understands in his or her own way).

But the healing is not quick or automatic. As one member of AA told me: "I walked twenty-six miles into the woods, and I need to walk another twenty-six miles to get out of the woods."

We retired people have the time to help each other heal by accompanying one another both into and out of the woods.

What wound did ever heal but by degrees?

—*William Shakespeare*

Generations

For almost thirty years I watched my two daughters interact with their two grandmothers. Maybe there's something to the idea that skipping generations builds magnificent relationships among family members. The interactions among these four females almost always made everyone involved better human beings.

One specific exchange became a repeated, loving mantra: "How's it feel to be beautiful?" "You ought to know!"

In retirement, we have the time to get to know the next generation once removed. Let's not lose the opportunity if it presents itself. We have a lot of grand things to offer one another.

The power to make others feel
good or bad about themselves
is the greatest power
in the world.

—*Anna Quindlen*

Ministry in Retirement

We tend to be so busy during our working and child-rearing years that we often have little time to get too involved with our parish or congregation.

But in retirement, our "now-and-then" service can become more regular and significant. We can be the ones who raise our hands when the pastor asks for help or we see a need that is not being filled.

We may have said goodbye to our paid jobs, but there is still plenty of work to be done. We can become "ministers in retirement" in our faith communities.

Ministry is a conscious choice—a vocation, if you will—that forms an important part of our Christian identity and life's work.

—*Mark G. Boyer*

Look At It This Way

There are two kinds of retirees in the world: the glass-half-full ones and the glass-half-empty ones. And no one irritates glass-half-empty people as much as glass-half-full people (and vice versa).

Do we focus on the effort or the reward, the price or the prize, the dark cloud or the silver lining?

Do we even remember we have a choice?

We can be sad that rose bushes have thorns or happy that thorn bushes have roses.

A Retirement Toast

"Nothing but the best!" That's the expected toast to anyone who is retiring. But shortly after Mom died I found this graceful prayer by an unknown author tucked into her prayer book. It might prove a more appropriate toast for most of us.

I do not wish you joy without sorrow.
Nor endless day without healing dark.
Nor brilliant sun without the restful shadow.
Nor tides that never turn against your bark.
I wish you faith and strength and love and wisdom—
goods golden enough to help some needy one.
I wish you songs but also blessed silence
and God's sweet peace when every day is done.

Elder Statespeople

No matter how perfect we'd like to be in retirement, we're bound to continue immature or counter-productive ways of acting that we hoped would simply disappear when we retired.

Still, the task of retirement is not to slip back into childish behavior or continue patterns we want to discard. Rather a "successful" retirement is one in which we work hard to become "elder statespeople" for our family and friends, hopefully without them even noticing how much we've changed!

It's not "old" behavior if I'm still doing it.

Selective Memory

Our memory is not a recollection of past events; our memory is a recollection of our perception of past events. So when we retirees go to judge the next generation, we should "remember when."

Remember when we thought we were invincible? Remember when we made compromises with our basic values? Remember when we thought we were making the world safe for everyone?

A less selective memory might make our generation a little more humble.

Thanks for the memories.

—Bob Hope

The Prayer Always Answered

I once heard a preacher say there's only one kind of prayer that's always answered: the prayer of gratitude. It's also the perfect prayer for us retirees, because we've got so much to be thankful for.

Thanks is the prayer that is always answered because the very act of saying "thank you" to God produces a very warm "you're welcome" in response. It's automatic.

Try it if you don't believe me.

If the only prayer you say in your whole life is "thank you," that would suffice.

—*Meister Eckhart*

Blessed Are Those Who Retire

No matter how aware of our blessings we try to be, it's almost impossible for those of us who are retired to truly realize how fortunate we are: me sitting here writing this little book and you sitting there reading it.

So when we're feeling low or when we're feeling high, it is still very good for us to remember how deeply advantaged we are compared to the vast majority of our fellow citizens of this planet.

We are retired or about to retire, and most people in history or alive today never got that opportunity.

I was born on third base and grew up
thinking I'd hit a triple.